SUPER CUTE!

Baby Elephants

by Christina Leaf

BELLWETHER MEDIA • MINNEAPOLIS, MN

Note to Librarians, Teachers, and Parents:

Blastoff! Readers are carefully developed by literacy experts and combine standards-based content with developmentally appropriate text.

Level 1 provides the most support through repetition of high-frequency words, light text, predictable sentence patterns, and strong visual support.

Level 2 offers early readers a bit more challenge through varied simple sentences, increased text load, and less repetition of high-frequency words.

Level 3 advances early-fluent readers toward fluency through increased text and concept load, less reliance on visuals, longer sentences, and more literary language.

Level 4 builds reading stamina by providing more text per page, increased use of punctuation, greater variation in sentence patterns, and increasingly challenging vocabulary.

Level 5 encourages children to move from "learning to read" to "reading to learn" by providing even more text, varied writing styles, and less familiar topics.

Whichever book is right for your reader, Blastoff! Readers are the perfect books to build confidence and encourage a love of reading that will last a lifetime!

This edition first published in 2015 by Bellwether Media, Inc.

Library of Congress Cataloging-in-Publication Data

Leaf, Christina, author.
Baby Elephants / by Christina Leaf.
pages cm. – (Blastoff! Readers. Super Cute!)
Summary: "Developed by literacy experts for students in kindergarten through grade three, this book introduces baby elephants to young readers through leveled text and related photos."– Provided by publisher.
Audience: Ages 5-8.
Audience: K to grade 3.
Includes bibliographical references and index.
ISBN 978-1-62617-169-5 (hardcover : alk. paper)
1. Elephants–Infancy–Juvenile literature. I. Title. II. Series: Blastoff! Readers. 1, Super Cute!
QL737.P98L43 2015
599.6713'92–dc23
2014034758

Printed in the United States of America, North Mankato, MN.

Table of Contents

Elephant Calf! 4
Life With Mom 6
Using the Trunk 16
Glossary 22
To Learn More 23
Index 24

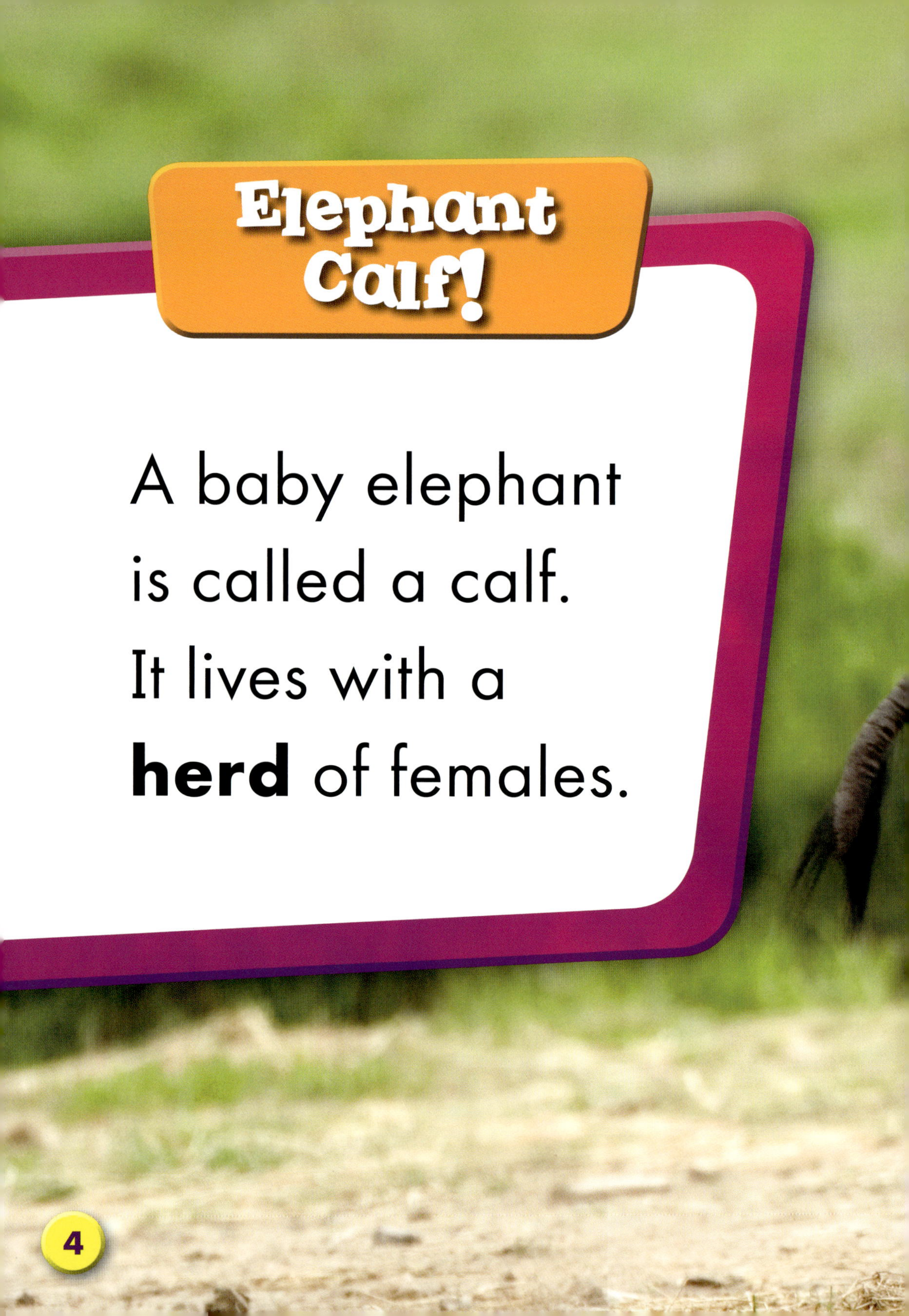

Elephant Calf!

A baby elephant is called a calf. It lives with a **herd** of females.

Life With Mom

The calf stays with the herd for at least two years. Mom cares for it.

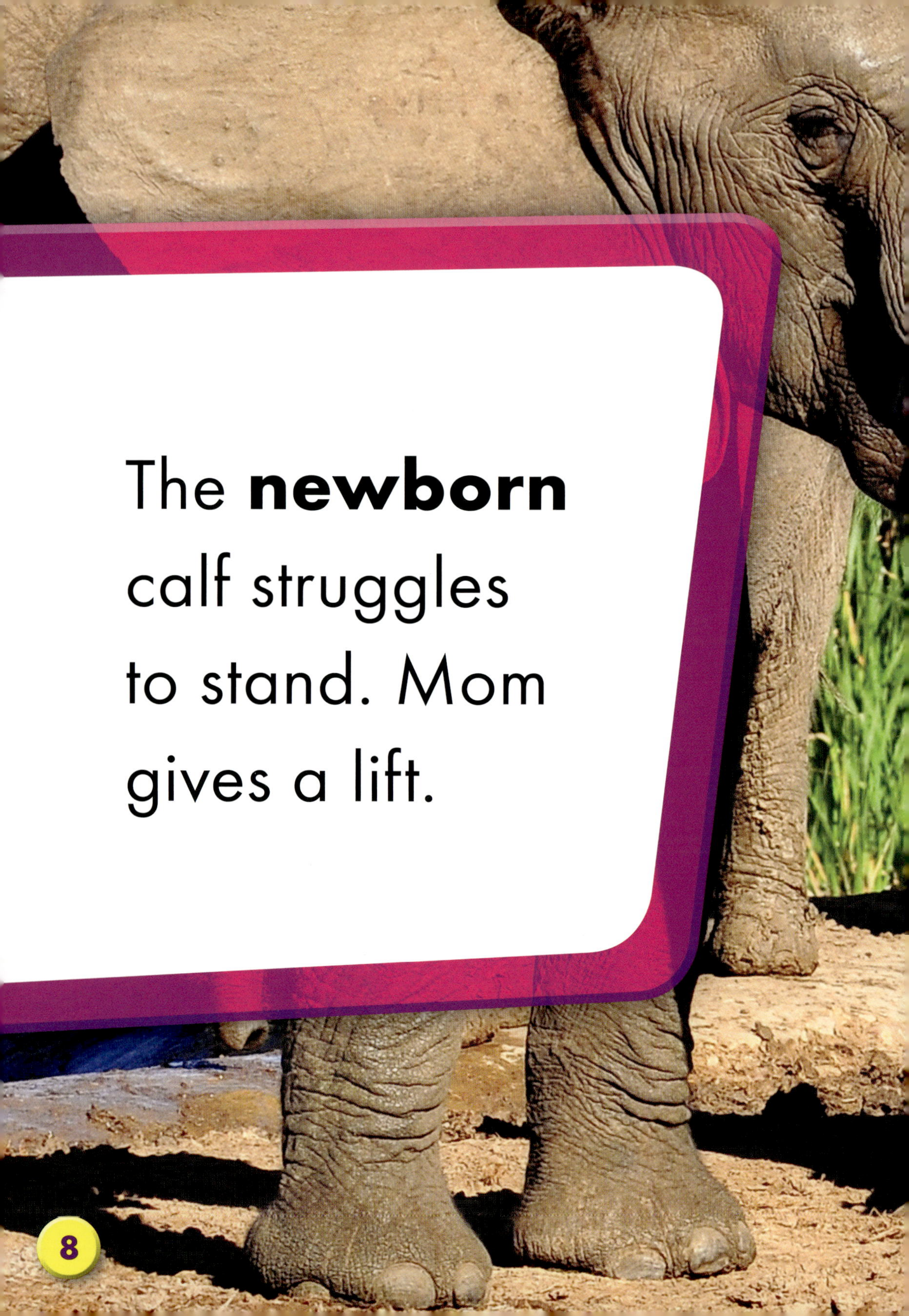

The **newborn** calf struggles to stand. Mom gives a lift.

The young calf drinks mom's milk for food.

It is time for a bath. Mom sprays the calf with her **trunk**.

The calf is in danger! Mom **trumpets** for help. The herd circles close.

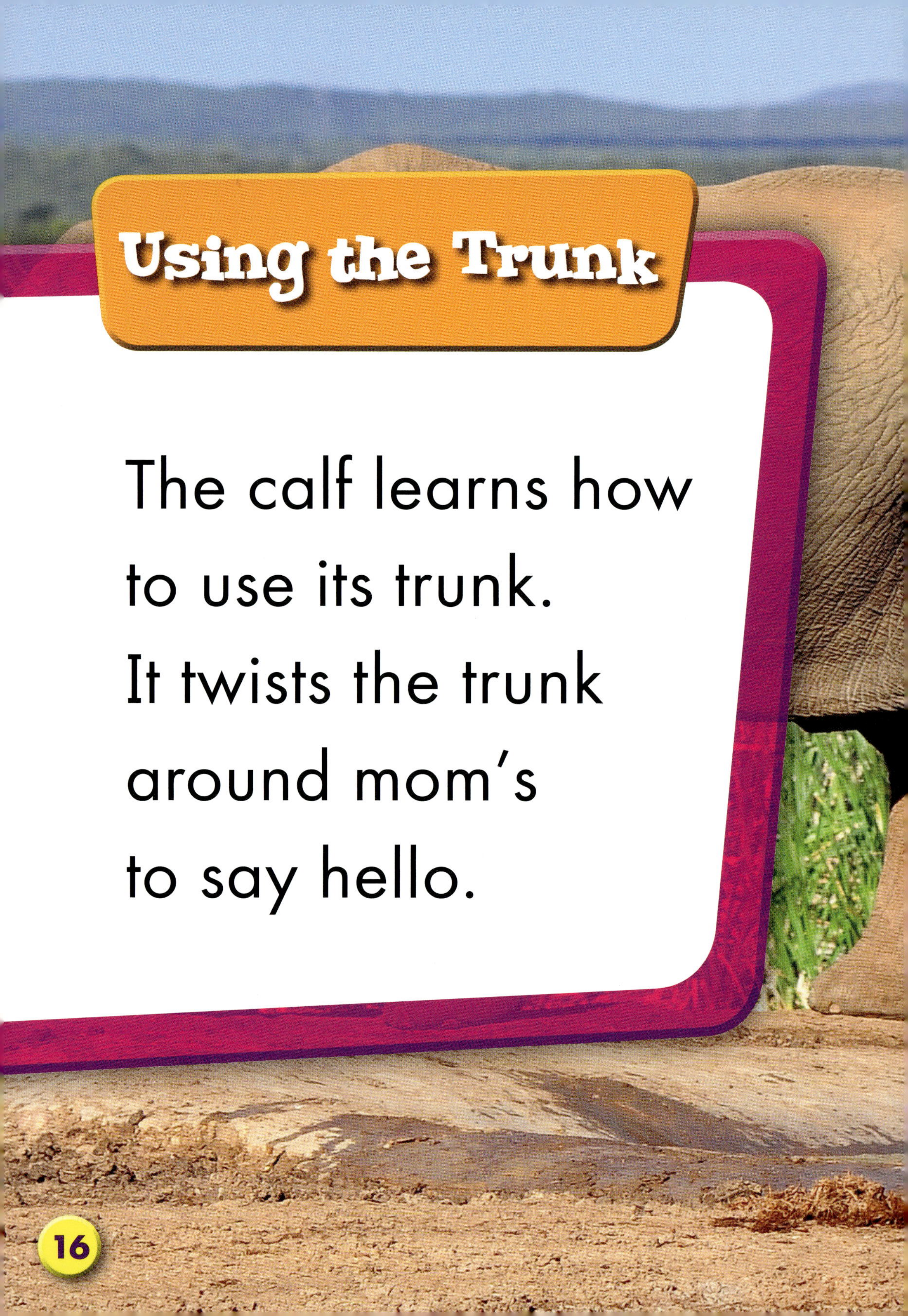

Using the Trunk

The calf learns how
to use its trunk.
It twists the trunk
around mom's
to say hello.

The calf watches how mom eats. It tries to pick up food with its trunk, too.

Sometimes the calf uses its trunk to hold mom's tail. This helps it stay close. Hold on tight!

Glossary

herd—a group of elephants that travel together

newborn—just recently born

trumpets—pushes air through the trunk to make a horn sound

trunk—the long nose and upper lip of an elephant

To Learn More

AT THE LIBRARY

Brunhoff, Jean de. *The Story of Babar, the Little Elephant.* New York, N.Y.: Random House, 2002.

Buckley, Carol. *Tarra & Bella: The Elephant and Dog Who Became Best Friends.* New York, N.Y.: G.P. Putnam's Sons, 2009.

Schuetz, Kari. *African Elephants.* Minneapolis, Minn.: Bellwether Media, 2012.

ON THE WEB

Learning more about elephants is as easy as 1, 2, 3.

1. Go to www.factsurfer.com.
2. Enter "elephants" into the search box.
3. Click the "Surf" button and you will see a list of related web sites.

With factsurfer.com, finding more information is just a click away.

Index

bath, 12
danger, 14
drinks, 10
eats, 18
females, 4
food, 10, 18
herd, 4, 6, 14
learns, 16
milk, 10
mom, 6, 8, 10, 12, 14, 16, 18, 20
newborn, 8
sprays, 12
stand, 8
tail, 20
trumpets, 14
trunk, 12, 16, 18, 20
twists, 16
watches, 18

The images in this book are reproduced through the courtesy of: Steve Bower, front cover; Penny Boyd/ Alamy, pp. 4-5; John Michael Evan Potter, pp. 6-7, 8-9, 10-11, 16-17; Four Oaks, pp. 12-13; Graeme Shannon, pp. 14-15; Alta Oosthuizen, pp. 18-19; Richard Wear/ Glow Images, pp. 20-21.